Contents

Snakes and their bodies 2
Tongues 4
Fangs 6
Big snakes and small snakes 8
Where snakes live 10
How snakes are born 14
Growing a new skin. 16
How snakes move 18
What snakes eat 20
Index 24

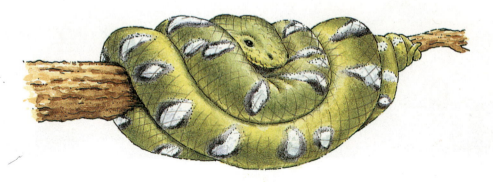

 # Snakes and their bodies

There are many kinds of snakes. All snakes are dangerous to animals. Some snakes are dangerous to humans, but most are not deadly to humans at all.

Every snake has a head, a body and a tail. Snakes do not have arms or legs.

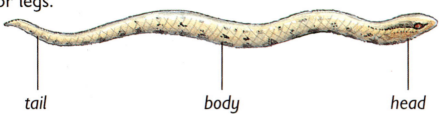

tail   body   head

Most snakes have eyes on the sides of their head. They cannot shut their eyes. They sleep with them open.

Snakes have eyes on the side of their head.

 # Tongues

A snake's tongue is split at the end. The tongue looks like a fork. The snake flicks its tongue in and out. It uses its tongue to smell where things are.

tongue

A snake's split tongue looks like a fork.

Snakes do not have ears, so they cannot hear sounds. Their bodies are on the ground and they feel the ground shake when something comes near.

Snakes feel the ground shake when something comes near.

 # Fangs

Some snakes have fangs in their jaws. The fangs are two sharp teeth. There can be poison in their fangs.

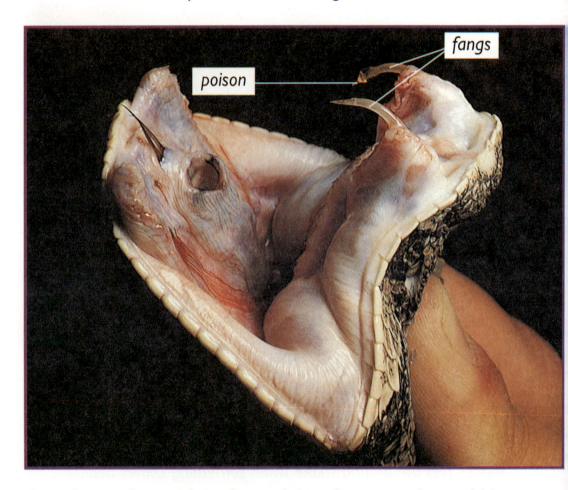

A snake can bite with its fangs. A bite from a snake could be deadly if there is poison in its fangs.

This rattlesnake is going to strike. When a snake is going to strike, it means that it is going to bite something. This rattlesnake's jaws are open. Can you see its fangs?

This rattlesnake is going to strike.

Big snakes and small snakes

Some snakes are very long and have thick bodies. This snake is an anaconda. The anaconda can be over seven metres long. It has a thick body so it is very heavy, too. It has black and yellow skin.

The anaconda is a very big snake.

Some snakes are very small. Small snakes have thin bodies.
This small snake is called a thread snake.
Can you see how long the thread snake is?

The thread snake is a very small snake.

Where snakes live

Snakes live in most parts of the world except very cold places. They cannot live in very cold places.

These snakes live in Britain. They are called the adder and the grass snake.

These snakes live in Britain.

Snakes live in all kinds of places. Some snakes live among rocks. Other snakes live in long grass.

This snake lives underground. It is called the blind snake.

The blind snake lives underground.

This snake lives up a tree. It is called a tree snake. It is green so that it can hide in the leaves. The tree snake eats eggs. It looks for birds' nests and eats the eggs in the nest.

The tree snake lives up a tree.

This is a sea snake. The sea snake lives in water. Sea snakes live in warm seas and eat fish.

The sea snake lives in warm seas.

 # How snakes are born

Most snakes lay eggs. The eggs have soft shells. The baby snake is inside the egg. It taps the shell with its tooth. The shell cracks and the baby snake crawls out.

A baby snake crawls out of its egg.

Some snakes do not lay eggs. This rattlesnake is having a baby. Can you see the baby snake? The baby snake is born in a bag of skin. It makes a hole in the skin and crawls out.

This rattlesnake is having a baby.

 # Growing a new skin

A snake's skin is dry and smooth. The skin is made of lots of small scales.

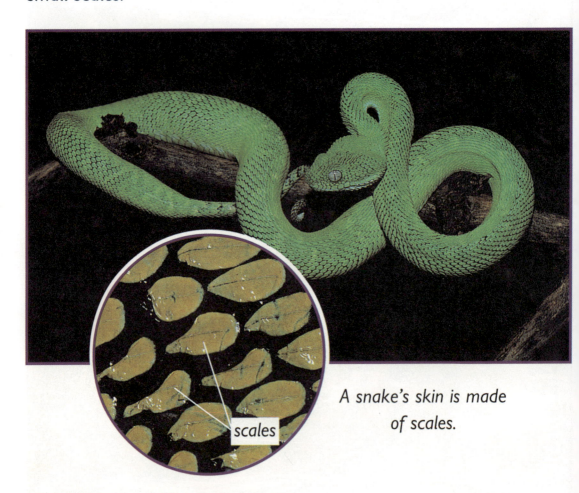

A snake's skin is made of scales.

As a snake grows, it grows a new skin. It grows a new skin five or six times a year.

This snake is changing its skin. It rubs its body on something hard. The old skin peels off and the snake crawls out. Its new skin is bright and clean.

This snake is changing its skin.

 # How snakes move

Snakes move by wriggling their bodies. They grip the ground with their scales. Then they push down on the ground. They wriggle along.

A snake moves by wriggling its body.

Most snakes can swim. This snake is swimming in a pond.

This is a flying tree snake. It can glide from tree to tree.

This tree snake can glide.

 # What snakes eat

Most snakes eat meat. Many snakes eat mice and rats. Some snakes even eat other snakes. This snake is eating a frog.

This snake is eating a frog.

Snakes cannot chew the food they eat. They swallow all of it. This snake is eating an egg. It cannot chew so it has to swallow the egg. It swallows the egg and then spits out the shell.

This snake is eating an egg.

This big snake is eating a deer. It twists its body around the deer and squeezes. It squeezes the deer very hard. Then it opens its jaws very wide. It swallows the deer.

A snake opens its jaws very wide to swallow a deer.

After a big meal, the snake is very fat. It finds a sunny place and curls up. It has a long rest. It will not eat again for weeks.

A snake has a rest after a meal.

Index

A
adder 10
anaconda 8

B
baby snakes 14, 15

E
eggs 12, 14, 15, 21

F
fangs 6, 7

G
grass snake 10

J
jaws 6, 7, 22

P
poison 6, 7

R
rattlesnake 6, 7, 15

S
scales 16, 18
sea snakes 13
skin 8, 15, 16, 17

T
thread snake 9
tree snake 12, 19